POLICE DOGS
PERROS POLICÍAS

Rosie Albright

Traducción al español: Eduardo Alamán

PowerKiDS press

New York

Published in 2012 by The Rosen Publishing Group, Inc.
29 East 21st Street, New York, NY 10010

First Edition

Editor: Joanne Randolph   Traducción al español: Eduardo Alamán
Book Design: Kate Laczynski

Photo Credits: Cover Jay Town/Newspix/Getty Images; pp. 5, 24 (right) Matt Cardy/Getty Images; p. 6 Matt King/Getty Images; pp. 8–9, 18, 20–21, 24 (left, center) Shutterstock.com; p. 10 Billy Hustace/Getty Images; p. 13 Justin Sullivan/Getty Images; pp. 14–15 Nicholas Kamm/ AFP/Getty Images; p. 17 Jim Frazee/Getty Images; p. 23 Mike Albans/NY Daily News Archive via Getty Images.

Library of Congress Cataloging-in-Publication Data

Albright, Rosie.
 Police dogs = Perros policías / by Rosie Albright. — 1st ed.
    p. cm. — (Animal detectives = Detectives del reino animal)
 Parallel title: Perros policías
 Parallel text in English and Spanish.
 Includes index.
 ISBN 978-1-4488-6714-1 (library binding)
 1. Police dogs—Juvenile literature. I. Title. II. Title: Perros policías.
 HV8025.A434 2012b
 363.2'32—dc23

                                        2011024634

Web Sites: Due to the changing nature of Internet links, PowerKids Press has developed an online list of Web sites related to the subject of this book. This site is updated regularly. Please use this link to access the list:
www.powerkidslinks.com/andt/dogs/

Manufactured in the United States of America

CPSIA Compliance Information: Batch #WW12PK: For Further Information contact Rosen Publishing, New York, New York at 1-800-237-9932

CONTENTS

CONTENIDO

Police dogs do important jobs. They work to keep people safe.

Los perros policías realizan tareas importantes. Los perros policía protegen a las personas.

MEDIA AREA
B

Police dogs work with a **handler**. An officer and dog are called a K-9 team.

Los perros policías trabajan con un **cuidador**. El equipo del oficial de policía y el perro se llama K-9.

The most common
kind of police dog is
the German shepherd.

La raza más común
de perro policía es el
pastor alemán.

Police dogs look for illegal things. They sniff out drugs and **bombs**.

Los perros policías buscan objetos ilegales. Los perros policías olfatean en busca de drogas y **bombas**.

Police dogs use their
noses to track people and
search buildings.

Los perros policías usan
su olfato para encontrar
personas y revisar edificios.

Dogs smell so well that they can smell a person who is under **rubble**. They can smell things buried underground, too.

Los perros tienen un buen olfato. Pueden oler a una persona atrapada entre los **escombros**. También pueden olfatear objetos enterrados.

Police dogs often wear special vests. The vests show they are working.

Con frecuencia, los perros policías usan chalecos especiales. Los chalecos muestran que el perro está trabajando.

The first K-9 units were trained in Belgium. One of the first American K-9 units was formed in Baltimore, Maryland.

El primer equipo K-9 se entrenó en Bélgica. En Estados Unidos las primeras unidades K-9 se formaron en Baltimore, Maryland.

Today many K-9 units train their dogs the same way Baltimore does. Running an **obstacle** course is one part of training.

Hoy, muchos equipos K-9 entrenan de la misma manera. Correr en una pista de **obstáculos** es parte del entrenamiento.

Police dogs are animal detectives. They are ready to help whenever they are needed.

Los perros policías son detectives del reino animal. Siempre están listos para ayudar cuando se les necesita.

Words to Know / Palabras que debes saber

bomb / (la) bomba

obstacle / (el) obstáculo

handler / (el/la) cuidador(a)

rubble / (los) escombros

24